Visit us at
www.adventuresofscubajack.com
for more FUN Learning!

Let's have some fun,
Beneath the bright sun!
We'll laugh, and we'll play,
All through the day!

Let's walk the dog,
Let's hunt for a frog.
We'll splash in the mud,
And jump with a thud!

Let's build a warm fire,
Its flames reaching higher.
Then into a balloon,
We'll soar past the moon!

Let's explore the backyard,
It's not very hard.
Look up at the star,
And dream from afar.

Cherish these moments and hold them so near.
Time slips away like a whisper we hear.
The laughter, the joy, the adventures we share,
Will live in our hearts as treasures so rare.

Be wild, be free, let each moment last,
Hold on to the joy, for time moves so fast.
They're the light of the world, their joy is the key
To the magic and wonder that's meant to be.

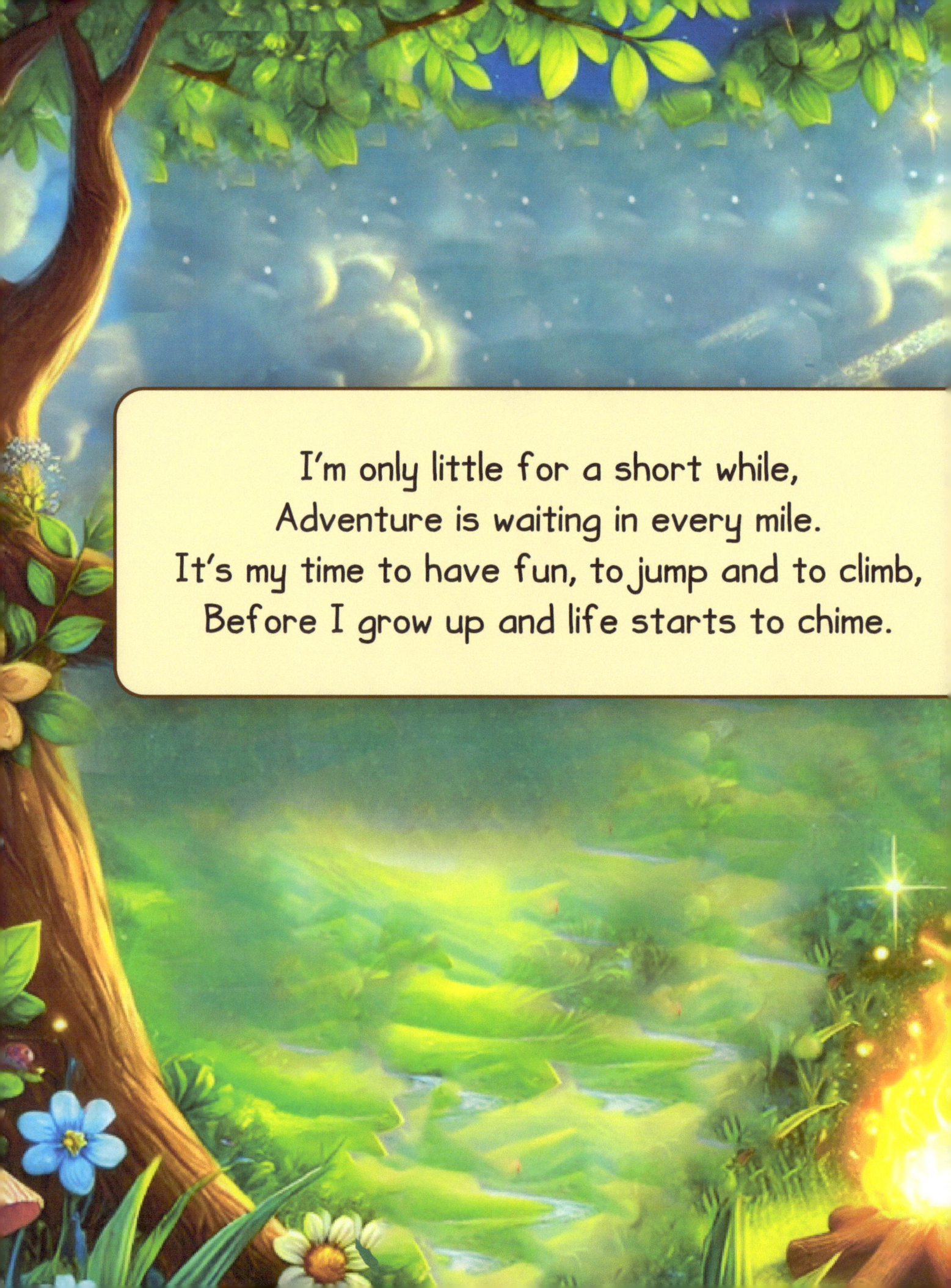

I'm only little for a short while,
Adventure is waiting in every mile.
It's my time to have fun, to jump and to climb,
Before I grow up and life starts to chime.

Let's climb every tree,
And live wild and free.
With all the wonders there are to see,
Let's explore this world, just you and me.

This is, "The Story of Fun," let it never fade.
In the hearts of all, the memories are made.
Hold on to the magic, the wonder, the play.
For life's greatest treasures are found each day